Morning Prayer, Rite II

Introduction

Morning and Evening Prayer are, with the Holy Eucharist, the most familiar services of the Book of Common Prayer, but they are very different in character from the Holy Eucharist. The Eucharist is primarily an action in which we are involved, and, to a degree, an end in itself. The Daily Offices (Morning and Evening Prayer), on the other hand, are more contemplative than active and are primarily a means for doing something else. They are intended to provide, first, a framework for our day and, second, a pattern for reading the Bible.

A Framework for the Day

Time is God's most elusive gift. There is no way to hold it or change it. But we can measure it and, indeed, one of the Psalms (104:20) suggests that God made the moon specifically to mark the seasons for us. If we can measure time, then we can also set aside a part of it to give back to God, just as we set aside parts of all our other gifts to offer them to the God who gives them to us. With time, as with money, we can find ways to set aside part as a way of showing that all of it belongs to God. The Sabbath was set aside as a way of making the whole week holy, and so we set aside times of daily prayer to mark each day as God's. This marking and offering of time to God is an act of both stewardship and praise.

Christians inherited a pattern of daily prayer from the Jews, who set aside three daily times of prayer. But Christians found the psalm verse (119:164) that says, "Seven times a day do I praise you" and by the Middle Ages monks had developed a tradition of seven daily times of prayer: Matins before dawn and Lauds at daybreak, which were combined into one service; then, at sunrise, midmorning, noon, and midafternoon were Prime, Terce, Sext, and None; Vespers came at sundown, and Compline at bedtime. Obviously, such a schedule could be kept only by monks and nuns, though lay people were encouraged to attend when they could.

In the first English Book of Common Prayer, in 1549, Archbishop Thomas Cranmer set out to combine and revise the Daily Offices ("office" from the Latin word for "duty") so that ordinary people could take part in them. The two new services of Morning Prayer and Evening Prayer would replace the sevenfold pattern and provide a way for everyone to praise God at the beginning and end of the day. These services, required for the clergy, did become so popular that for centuries they pushed aside the eucharist and even became the principal Sunday services, morning and evening. The eucharist having been restored to its central place, Morning and Evening Prayer, in their turn, have often been pushed aside. As a remedy, the 1979 Prayer Book offers brief "Daily Devotions" for morning, noon, early evening, and close of day (pages 136-140) and also restores the service of Compline to assist Christians who want a structure of prayer for their daily lives.

A User's Guide to the Book of Common Prayer

Morning Prayer I and II and Holy Baptism

Christopher L. Webber

MOREHOUSE PUBLISHING

Morehouse Publishing
P.O. Box 1321
Harrisburg, PA 17105

A catalog record for this book is available from the Library of Congress.

Printed in the United States of America

Contents

NOTE: Complete commentary is provided only for Rite II Morning Prayer because it includes more material than does Rite I. In particular, it includes 14 Canticles instead of seven. The commentary on Rite I discusses only the differences between the two rites. The Rite II commentary can be used for information about all of the material in Rite I.

In the 1979 Book of Common Prayer the basic structure of Morning and Evening Prayer remains essentially unchanged from Cranmer's pattern. Traditional and contemporary language versions (Rite I and Rite II) are provided. Whether we take part in the services in a cathedral or parish church or say them at home, in an office, on a commuter train, or elsewhere, the goal of sanctifying time by framing each day with prayer remains the same: to provide opportunity for every Christian to offer each day to God.

A Pattern for Reading the Bible

Part of the original purpose of the monastic offices was to allow the Bible to be read through in some systematic way. In the middle ages the growing number of saints days interrupted the regular pattern of readings, and one of Archbishop Cranmer's objectives was to enable lay people to hear the whole Bible read.

Central to both Morning and Evening Prayer are the readings from the Bible. In Cranmer's plan, there was to be one reading from the Old Testament and one from the New at each service. Most of the Old Testament and the Apocrypha would be read through each year, and the New Testament (except for the Book of Revelation) was to be read through three times each year. The psalms were divided into sixty portions with the purpose of reading daily portions morning and evening and so using all the psalms once each month.

The 1979 Prayer Book allows for the use of the thirty-day cycle of psalm readings but also provides a schedule that distributes the psalms over seven weeks through most of the year. Three lessons, one each from the Old Testament, the Epistles, and the Gospels, are provided for each day with the intention that two be read in the morning and one in the evening. Following this pattern, most of the Old Testament would be read through in two years and most of the New Testament every year. Alternatives include reading three lessons at one service daily or two lessons at both daily services.

The readings from the Bible are preceded by the psalms and separated and followed by Canticles. These provide opportunity to reflect on the readings while they are said or sung and to respond to the readings with praise. The readings and Canticles are followed by the Apostles' Creed and prayers, so that the readings lead to a statement of faith and the service then concludes with prayer. Morning and Evening Prayer are, then, biblical services: a way to read the Bible in a careful and systematic way as part of an offering of praise and prayer by the Christian community.

Just as the monastic offices were usually sung, so Morning and Evening Prayer have developed a rich heritage of music. Music adds to the beauty of the service, but there is also a very practical advantage to singing. Chanting the psalms and Canticles makes it easier to recite them in unison, and chanting the prayers makes it easier to hear the words, especially in a large church or cathedral. Evening Prayer, especially, is so often sung that it has frequently been known as "Evensong." But while the Daily Offices may be elaborately sung, they may also be recited very simply by a few people in a small chapel or said privately by an individual with a Bible and a Prayer Book and ten or fifteen quiet minutes. So doing frames our time in a Bible centered pattern of prayer, shared in by countless Christians throughout the world.

How to Use Morning (and Evening) Prayer

For most Christians daily attendance at church morning and evening will be impractical, but the Daily Offices can be used at home (before breakfast or after dinner, for example) or in the office or while traveling. Longer and shorter versions can be used, as follows.

1 - Full Morning Prayer (Rite II)

Opening sentences (choose one or more)   pages 75-78
Invitatory   page 80
Canticle (*Venite* or *Jubilate*, except *Christ our Passover* at Easter time)   pages 82-83
Psalm (selections listed on pages 936 ff., or use the psalms for the day of the month from page 585 ff.)
First Lesson (selections listed on page 936 ff., or begin with Genesis and read a chapter a day)
Canticle (choose one)   pages 85-95
Second Lesson (selections on p. 936 ff. or begin with St. Matthew and read a chapter a day)
The Apostles' Creed   page 96
The Prayers (Lord's Prayer and Suffrages from page 97, one collect from pages 98-100, one prayer from pages 100-101, other prayers optional)
Conclusion   page 102

2 - A Shorter Version of Morning Prayer (Rite II)

Opening sentences (choose one or more)   pages 75-78
Invitatory   page 80
Canticle (*Venite* or *Jubilate*, except *Christ our*
    Passover at Easter time)   pages 82-83
Psalm (selections listed on pages 936 ff., or use the
    psalms for the day of the month from page 585 ff.)
One Lesson (selections listed on page 936 ff., or begin
    with Genesis or St. Matthew and read a chapter a day)
The Apostles' Creed   page 96
The Prayers (page 97, one collect from pages 98-100,
    one prayer from pages 100-101, other prayers optional)
Conclusion   page 102

The Daily Office

Daily Morning Prayer: Rite Two

The Officiant begins the service with one or more of these sentences of Scripture, or with the versicle "Lord, open our lips" on page 80.

Advent

Watch, for you do not know when the master of the house will come, in the evening, or at midnight, or at cockcrow, or in the morning, lest he come suddenly and find you asleep. *Mark 13:35, 36*

In the wilderness prepare the way of the Lord, make straight in the desert a highway for our God.   *Isaiah 40:3*

The glory of the Lord shall be revealed, and all flesh shall see it together.   *Isaiah 40:5*

Christmas

Behold, I bring you good news of a great joy which will come to all the people; for to you is born this day in the city of David, a Savior, who is Christ the Lord.   *Luke 2:10, 11*

Behold, the dwelling of God is with mankind. He will dwell with them, and they shall be his people, and God himself will be with them, and be their God.   *Revelation 21:3*

Commentary

Daily Morning Prayer

The title makes it clear that this is a daily morning service. The word *prayer* is used in the broadest sense as a synonym for *worship*. General directions on page 74 of the Prayer Book indicate that the service may be led by anyone, ordained or not, and that it is appropriate to assign other individuals to read the lessons.

Opening Sentences
Since this is a service that centers on the reading of Scripture, the service appropriately begins with the reading of one or more sentences from the Bible. The service can also begin (as Cranmer's first version of the Prayer Book did) with the words "Lord, open our lips" found on page 80. When Cranmer added the opening sentences in 1552, they were all of a penitential nature and led into a General Confession. Beginning with the first American Prayer Book in 1789, a greater variety of sentences has been provided so that now there are sentences for every season of the Church Year as well as "Occasions of Thanksgiving" and sentences to be used "At any Time." Since the Confession is now optional, these sentences can lead appropriately to the Invitatory. The only penitential sentences remaining are those designated for Lent.

Epiphany

Nations shall come to your light, and kings to the brightness of your rising.   *Isaiah 60:3*

I will give you as a light to the nations, that my salvation may reach to the end of the earth.   *Isaiah 49:6b*

From the rising of the sun to its setting my Name shall be great among the nations, and in every place incense shall be offered to my Name, and a pure offering; for my Name shall be great among the nations, says the Lord of hosts.   *Malachi 1:11*

Lent

If we say we have no sin, we deceive ourselves, and the truth is not in us, but if we confess our sins, God, who is faithful and just, will forgive our sins and cleanse us from all unrighteousness.   *1 John 1:8, 9*

Rend your hearts and not your garments. Return to the Lord your God, for he is gracious and merciful, slow to anger and abounding in steadfast love, and repents of evil.   *Joel 2:13*

I will arise and go to my father, and I will say to him, "Father, I have sinned against heaven and before you; I am no longer worthy to be called your son."   *Luke 15:18, 19*

To the Lord our God belong mercy and forgiveness, because we have rebelled against him and have not obeyed the voice of the Lord our God by following his laws which he set before us.   *Daniel 9:9, 10*

Jesus said, "If anyone would come after me, let him deny himself and take up his cross and follow me."   *Mark 8:34*

Holy Week

All we like sheep have gone astray; we have turned every one

The purpose of the opening sentences is to begin with a verse of the Bible to provide the keynote of the service. The great number of sentences provided illustrates the perennial conflict between variety and sameness.

The Daily Offices are intended to sanctify our time. Is it more important to notice what is special about this particular day or to establish a pattern so unchanging that it can be said from memory? Obviously there are advantages either way. Perhaps the best solution is for individuals to settle on a sentence that changes only with the great seasons and major holy days if at all, while making use of the rich variety provided here for larger services and special occasions. Routine may be what matters for individuals and small communities; too much variety can result in wondering why a sentence was chosen and breaking the participants' concentration. It may even be good to go straight to "Lord, open our lips" so that we are immediately involved in dialogue with God. Variety, on the other hand, can add to the special character of larger gatherings. Then sentences can be chosen to keynote the occasion.

Notice that the Easter Season sentences include one appropriate for Ascension Day and one appropriate for Pentecost.

to his own way; and the Lord has laid on him the iniquity of us all.   *Isaiah 53:6*

Is it nothing to you, all you who pass by? Look and see if there is any sorrow like my sorrow which was brought upon me, whom the Lord has afflicted.   *Lamentations 1:12*

Easter Season, including Ascension Day
and the Day of Pentecost

Alleluia! Christ is risen.
The Lord is risen indeed. Alleluia!

On this day the Lord has acted; we will rejoice and be glad in it.   *Psalm 118:24*

Thanks be to God, who gives us the victory through our Lord Jesus Christ.   *1 Corinthians 15:57*

If then you have been raised with Christ, seek the things that are above, where Christ is, seated at the right hand of God. *Colossians 3:1*

Christ has entered, not into a sanctuary made with hands, a copy of the true one, but into heaven itself, now to appear in the presence of God on our behalf.   *Hebrews 9:24*

You shall receive power when the Holy Spirit has come upon you; and you shall be my witnesses in Jerusalem, and in all Judea, and Samaria, and to the ends of the earth.   *Acts 1:8*

Trinity Sunday

Holy, holy, holy is the Lord God Almighty, who was, and is, and is to come!   *Revelation 4:8*

All Saints and other Major Saints' Days

We give thanks to the Father, who has made us worthy to share in the inheritance of the saints in light.   *Colossians 1:12*

You are no longer strangers and sojourners, but fellow citizens with the saints and members of the household of God.   *Ephesians 2:19*

Their sound has gone out into all lands, and their message to the ends of the world.   *Psalm 19:4*

Occasions of Thanksgiving

Give thanks to the Lord, and call upon his Name; make known his deeds among the peoples.   *Psalm 105:1*

At any Time

Grace to you and peace from God our Father and the Lord Jesus Christ.   *Philippians 1:2*

I was glad when they said to me, "Let us go to the house of the Lord."   *Psalm 122:1*

Let the words of my mouth and the meditation of my heart be acceptable in your sight, O Lord, my strength and my redeemer.   *Psalm 19:14*

Send out your light and your truth, that they may lead me, and bring me to your holy hill and to your dwelling.
Psalm 43:3

The Lord is in his holy temple; let all the earth keep silence before him.   *Habakkuk 2:20*

The hour is coming, and now is, when the true worshipers will worship the Father in spirit and truth, for such the Father seeks to worship him.   *John 4:23*

Thus says the high and lofty One who inhabits eternity, whose name is Holy, "I dwell in the high and holy place and also with the one who has a contrite and humble spirit, to revive the spirit of the humble and to revive the heart of the contrite."   *Isaiah 57:15*

The following Confession of Sin may then be said; or the Office may continue at once with "Lord, open our lips."

Confession of Sin

The Officiant says to the people

Dearly beloved, we have come together in the presence of Almighty God our heavenly Father, to set forth his praise, to hear his holy Word, and to ask, for ourselves and on behalf of others, those things that are necessary for our life and our salvation. And so that we may prepare ourselves in heart and mind to worship him, let us kneel in silence, and with penitent and obedient hearts confess our sins, that we may obtain forgiveness by his infinite goodness and mercy.

or this

Let us confess our sins against God and our neighbor.

Silence may be kept.

Officiant and People together, all kneeling

Most merciful God,
we confess that we have sinned against you
in thought, word, and deed,
by what we have done,
and by what we have left undone.
We have not loved you with our whole heart;
we have not loved our neighbors as ourselves.
We are truly sorry and we humbly repent.
For the sake of your Son Jesus Christ,
have mercy on us and forgive us;
that we may delight in your will,
and walk in your ways,
to the glory of your Name. Amen.

Confession of Sin

The Confession of Sin has three sections: a bidding or invitation, the confession itself, and the absolution. The bidding (which might appropriately be preceded at any time by one of the Lenten opening sentences) has both a long and a short alternative form. The longer bidding sets out the purpose of the whole service: to praise God, to hear God's Word, and to ask for ourselves and for others. The confession is then provided as a way to prepare ourselves to take part in this service.

Here and throughout the service times of silence are suggested for individual reflection. The silence before the confession allows opportunity to recall our failures so that we can ask God's forgiveness for them.

The confession lists briefly the ways in which we fall short of our calling: by our thoughts, words, and actions, both done and left undone. In a busy world, we are all aware of the items remaining on our "to do" lists, but we ought to think as well of the actions that never get on our lists at all. How much of what we are aware of having left undone doesn't really need to be done, and how many other good things might we have done for God and others if we had loved God more?

Almighty God have mercy on you, forgive you all your sins through our Lord Jesus Christ, strengthen you in all goodness, and by the power of the Holy Spirit keep you in eternal life. *Amen.*

A deacon or lay person using the preceding form remains kneeling, and substitutes "us" for "you" and "our" for "your."

The Invitatory and Psalter

All stand

Officiant	Lord, open our lips.
People	And our mouth shall proclaim your praise.

Officiant and People

Glory to the Father, and to the Son, and to the Holy Spirit: as it was in the beginning, is now, and will be for ever. Amen.

Except in Lent, add   Alleluia.

Then follows one of the Invitatory Psalms, Venite or Jubilate.

One of the following Antiphons may be sung or said with the Invitatory Psalm

In Advent

Our King and Savior now draws near: Come let us adore him.

On the Twelve Days of Christmas

Alleluia. To us a child is born: Come let us adore him. Alleluia.

The absolution flows from the fact that it is God's nature to have mercy and moves on from pronouncing forgiveness to provide also the strength to live a new life and to continue in the risen, eternal life given us in baptism but constantly in need of renewal. Forgiveness is not simply to deal with the past, but also to enable us to move into the future to which God calls us.

Notice that the absolution can be modified into a declaration of forgiveness when no bishop or priest is present by changing "you" and "your" to "us" and "our."

The Invitatory and Psalter

The Invitatory in the monastic office consisted of a set psalm and antiphon. Here the term is broadened to include the whole section from the opening sentences and confession to the psalms and readings. This may also be the opening movement of the service. Either way, it invites us to join in praise of God.

"Lord, open our lips" was the beginning of the monastic office and may still be used to open the service. That verse and response are followed by two brief but powerful formulas that occur frequently in the Prayer Book: the "Gloria" and the "Alleluia."

The *Gloria*, or *Gloria Patri*, is a one-sentence summary of Christian worship that can be traced to the fourth century and may have been suggested originally by the baptismal formula: "In the Name of the Father and of the Son and of the Holy Spirit." It has traditionally been used at the end of each psalm or all the psalms and in other places as well.

*From the Epiphany through the Baptism of Christ, and on the Feasts of
the Transfiguration and Holy Cross*

The Lord has shown forth his glory: Come let us adore him.

In Lent

The Lord is full of compassion and mercy: Come let us
adore him.

From Easter Day until the Ascension

Alleluia. The Lord is risen indeed: Come let us adore him.
Alleluia.

From Ascension Day until the Day of Pentecost

Alleluia. Christ the Lord has ascended into heaven: Come
let us adore him. Alleluia.

On the Day of Pentecost

Alleluia. The Spirit of the Lord renews the face of the earth:
Come let us adore him. Alleluia.

On Trinity Sunday

Father, Son, and Holy Spirit, one God: Come let us adore him.

On other Sundays and Weekdays

The earth is the Lord's for he made it: Come let us adore him.

or this

Worship the Lord in the beauty of holiness: Come let us
adore him.

or this

The mercy of the Lord is everlasting: Come let us adore him.

The word *Alleluia* is a Christianized version of the Hebrew word *Hallelujah* (still used, of course, by Christians also and used in the 1979 Prayer Book version of the psalms), which means "praise God." This word is traditionally never used in Lent so that it comes with special force when its use is restored at Easter.

Antiphons are verses of Scripture used as a refrain with psalms or Canticles. The seasonal and general antiphons can be used at the beginning and end of the fixed psalm or Canticle, as well as between the three sections of that reading. The antiphon can provide a simple congregational response which would be especially useful if there is an elaborate musical setting.

The Alleluias in the following Antiphons are used only in Easter Season.

On Feasts of the Incarnation

[Alleluia.] The Word was made flesh and dwelt among us:
Come let us adore him. [Alleluia.]

On All Saints and other Major Saints' Days

[Alleluia.] The Lord is glorious in his saints: Come let us
adore him. [Alleluia.]

Venite   *Psalm 95:1-7*

Come, let us sing to the Lord; *
   let us shout for joy to the Rock of our salvation.
Let us come before his presence with thanksgiving *
   and raise a loud shout to him with psalms.

For the Lord is a great God, *
   and a great King above all gods.
In his hand are the caverns of the earth, *
   and the heights of the hills are his also.
The sea is his, for he made it, *
   and his hands have molded the dry land.

Come, let us bow down, and bend the knee, *
   and kneel before the Lord our Maker.
For he is our God,
and we are the people of his pasture and the sheep of his hand. *
   Oh, that today you would hearken to his voice!

or Psalm 95, page 724.

Jubilate   *Psalm 100*

Be joyful in the Lord, all you lands; *
   serve the Lord with gladness
   and come before his presence with a song.

A choice of three Invitatory Canticles is provided, though the third choice is ordinarily used only in Easter Season. The Prayer Book says that metrical versions (arranged for singing to hymn tunes) of the Invitatory Psalms and the Canticles may be used and a collection of metrical Canticles and psalms is available from Church Publishing. This might be especially helpful in small congregations with limited musical reources.

Venite

The *Venite* is a shortened version of Psalm 95 which seems to have been written for use in worship at the Temple in Jerusalem. For at least 2,500 years it has summoned God's people to worship. The earliest versions of the Daily Office include this psalm for the first office of the day. While the *Venite* does speak of the "God of our salvation," emphasis is on God revealed in nature. God is known to us first as Creator, and it is the wonder of creation that we are made aware of with each returning day. It is the order and beauty and rhythmic pattern of nature that provide the first motivation for the regularity of the daily offering of prayer. Many believe that no better invitation to praise and worship than the *Venite* has ever been written. The whole of Psalm 95, with its warning against "hardening your hearts," may be used at any time and should be used on Fridays in Lent.

Know this: The Lord himself is God; *
    he himself has made us, and we are his;
    we are his people and the sheep of his pasture.

Enter his gates with thanksgiving;
go into his courts with praise; *
    give thanks to him and call upon his Name.

For the Lord is good;
his mercy is everlasting; *
    and his faithfulness endures from age to age.

In Easter Week, in place of an Invitatory Psalm, the following is sung or said. It may also be used daily until the Day of Pentecost.

Christ our Passover   *Pascha nostrum*

1 Corinthians 5:7-8; Romans 6:9-11; 1 Corinthians 15:20-22

Alleluia.
Christ our Passover has been sacrificed for us; *
    therefore let us keep the feast,
Not with the old leaven, the leaven of malice and evil, *
    but with the unleavened bread of sincerity and truth. Alleluia.

Christ being raised from the dead will never die again; *
    death no longer has dominion over him.
The death that he died, he died to sin, once for all; *
    but the life he lives, he lives to God.
So also consider yourselves dead to sin, *
    and alive to God in Jesus Christ our Lord. Alleluia.

Christ has been raised from the dead, *
    the first fruits of those who have fallen asleep.
For since by a man came death, *
    by a man has come also the resurrection of the dead.
For as in Adam all die, *
    so also in Christ shall all be made alive. Alleluia.

Jubilate

As the *Venite* was a fixed part of Matins, so the *Jubilate* (Psalm 100) was part of Lauds and Prime. Both Canticles speak of us as God's "people . . . and . . . sheep." Paraphrased as "All people that on earth do dwell" and "Before the Lord's eternal throne,"* it has been among the most popular of Christian hymns. The tune written by Louis Bourgeois for the metrical version of Psalm 100 and known as Old Hundredth is perhaps the most familiar hymn tune in Protestant hymnody and is said to be the only tune preserved intact from the time of the Reformation.

Christ our Passover

The Canticle, *Christ our Passover*, was constructed by Archbishop Cranmer for use in the Easter procession and is made up of passages from St. Paul's epistles to the churches in Rome and Corinth that proclaim the resurrection. As already stated, "Alleluia" is a shout of praise inherited from the Jewish "Hallelujah" or "praise Yahweh." Christians associate it especially with the celebration of Easter.

*The original line, by John Wesley, was "Before Jehovah's awful throne," but most recent hymnals change the wording somehow because *awful* no longer means "full of awe."

Then follows

The Psalm or Psalms Appointed

At the end of the Psalms is sung or said

Glory to the Father, and to the Son, and to the Holy Spirit: *
    as it was in the beginning, is now, and will be for ever. Amen.

The Lessons

One or two Lessons, as appointed, are read, the Reader first saying

A Reading (Lesson) from _____ .

A citation giving chapter and verse may be added.

After each Lesson the Reader may say

    The Word of the Lord.
Answer   Thanks be to God.

Or the Reader may say   Here ends the Lesson (Reading).

Silence may be kept after each Reading. One of the following Canticles, or one of those on pages 47-52 (Canticles 1-7), is sung or said after each Reading. If three Lessons are used, the Lesson from the Gospel is read after the second Canticle.

The Psalm or Psalms Appointed

The psalms are the great hymn book of Judaism and Christianity alike. Many of the most familiar Christian hymns are simply paraphrases of psalms. No other poem has been as widely used and loved as Psalm 23 and Psalms 1, 15, 95, 100, and 150 are almost as valued. The psalms run the gamut of human emotion, from grief and doubt and anger to joy and praise. Regular and frequent use of the psalms makes them part of our vocabulary, available to help us speak to God whatever the need or occasion. Note the directions on pages 582-584 concerning the ways in which the psalms can be said and the importance of making a distinct pause at the asterisk for the sake of rhythm and meaning

The Lessons

The Lessons are the heart of the Daily Office: God's Word addressing us in a context of prayer and praise. It is a temptation for Christians to select favorite passages rather than read the whole Bible in a disciplined way. The medieval church had gradually shortened the passages read in its services to a few verses at a time, so Cranmer set out to restore the reading of the whole Bible. Revised many times since Cranmer's day, the lectionary (table of readings) still has the same goal. On pages 936-1001 readings are suggested for every day of the year in a two-year cycle and for special occasions as well (Year One in odd-numbered years and Year Two in even-numbered years), but these selections are also incomplete. Especially if Christians are reading the Office privately, they might find it preferable to read through the Bible a chapter at time or one chapter each of the Old and New Testaments, so that the whole Bible will be read and they will gain context and perspective. Note also that provision is made for reading one, two, or three passages with either Office.

8 The Song of Moses *Cantemus Domino*

Exodus 15:1-6, 11-13, 17-18

Especially suitable for use in Easter Season

I will sing to the Lord, for he is lofty and uplifted; *
    the horse and its rider has he hurled into the sea.
The Lord is my strength and my refuge; *
    the Lord has become my Savior.
This is my God and I will praise him, *
    the God of my people and I will exalt him.
The Lord is a mighty warrior; *
    Yahweh is his Name.
The chariots of Pharaoh and his army has he hurled into the sea; *
    the finest of those who bear armor have been
                   drowned in the Red Sea.
The fathomless deep has overwhelmed them; *
    they sank into the depths like a stone.
Your right hand, O Lord, is glorious in might; *
    your right hand, O Lord, has overthrown the enemy.
Who can be compared with you, O Lord, among the gods? *
    who is like you, glorious in holiness,
    awesome in renown, and worker of wonders?
You stretched forth your right hand; *
    the earth swallowed them up.
With your constant love you led the people you redeemed; *
    with your might you brought them in safety to
                   your holy dwelling.
You will bring them in and plant them *
    on the mount of your possession,
The resting-place you have made for yourself, O Lord, *
    the sanctuary, O Lord, that your hand has established.
The Lord shall reign *
    for ever and for ever.

Glory to the Father, and to the Son, and to the Holy Spirit: *
    as it was in the beginning, is now, and will be for ever. Amen.

Canticles

The reading of each lesson is followed by a Canticle, an ancient hymn from the Bible or the early church or one of the psalms. Fourteen are provided on pages 85-96, but the traditional-language versions of many of them (pages 47-53) can also be used. A suggested plan for using all the Canticles in turn is provided on page 144. Some of the Canticles are associated with certain seasons, and usually the Old Testament Canticles (8-14) will be more appropriate after the first reading, and the Canticles from the New Testament and early church will fit better after New Testament readings.

8 The Song of Moses

The song of victory celebrating the Jewish escape from slavery in Egypt became a part of the Easter Vigil service at an early date and then found its way into other medieval services. Because the 1979 Prayer Book places such stress on the centrality of Easter, this Canticle has been provided with the suggestion that it is most appropriate in Easter Season.

9   The First Song of Isaiah   *Ecce, Deus*
Isaiah 12:2-6

Surely, it is God who saves me; *
   I will trust in him and not be afraid.
For the Lord is my stronghold and my sure defense, *
   and he will be my Savior.
Therefore you shall draw water with rejoicing *
   from the springs of salvation.
And on that day you shall say, *
   Give thanks to the Lord and call upon his Name;
Make his deeds known among the peoples; *
   see that they remember that his Name is exalted.
Sing the praises of the Lord, for he has done great things, *
   and this is known in all the world.
Cry aloud, inhabitants of Zion, ring out your joy, *
   for the great one in the midst of you is the Holy One of Israel.

Glory to the Father, and to the Son, and to the Holy Spirit: *
   as it was in the beginning, is now, and will be for ever. Amen.

10   The Second Song of Isaiah   *Quærite Dominum*
Isaiah 55:6-11

Seek the Lord while he wills to be found; *
   call upon him when he draws near.
Let the wicked forsake their ways *
   and the evil ones their thoughts;
And let them turn to the Lord, and he will have compassion, *
   and to our God, for he will richly pardon.
For my thoughts are not your thoughts, *
   nor your ways my ways, says the Lord.
For as the heavens are higher than the earth, *
   so are my ways higher than your ways,
   and my thoughts than your thoughts.

9, 10, and 11 The First, Second, and Third Songs of Isaiah
These three Canticles have not been included in any previous version
of the Prayer Book (except the *Third Song* in a recent Canadian Prayer
Book) but are found in some medieval and eastern office books and
liturgies. These are some of the many psalms found not in the Book
of Psalms but in one of the prophets. Giving thanks as they do for
God's saving strength and victory, they make an appropriate
response to many passages from the Bible. Like Canticles 12, 14, 18,
and 19, they have been translated by Dr. Charles Guilbert.

12 and 13 A Song of Creation and A Song of Praise
These two Canticles (in reverse order) were later additions to the
Book of Daniel and are found now in the Apocrypha. They are a
paraphrase of Psalm 148 and are said to be the song sung by the
three men thrown into the fiery furnace by King Nebuchadnezzar
(see Daniel 3). These songs have always been popular among
Christians and have been in the Book of Common Prayer since 1549.

14 A Song of Penitence
This Canticle also is from the Apocrypha but was composed to add
Manasseh's prayer of repentance to the account in 2 Chronicles 33.
It has some previous history of liturgical use, but not in the Book of
Common Prayer before 1979. As a prayer of penitence it is especially
appropriate in Lent.

For as rain and snow fall from the heavens *
　　and return not again, but water the earth,
Bringing forth life and giving growth, *
　　seed for sowing and bread for eating,
So is my word that goes forth from my mouth; *
　　it will not return to me empty;
But it will accomplish that which I have purposed, *
　　and prosper in that for which I sent it.

Glory to the Father, and to the Son, and to the Holy Spirit: *
　　as it was in the beginning, is now, and will be for ever. Amen.

11 The Third Song of Isaiah *Surge, illuminare*
Isaiah 60:1-3, 11a, 14c, 18-19

Arise, shine, for your light has come, *
　　and the glory of the Lord has dawned upon you.
For behold, darkness covers the land; *
　　deep gloom enshrouds the peoples.
But over you the Lord will rise, *
　　and his glory will appear upon you.
Nations will stream to your light, *
　　and kings to the brightness of your dawning.
Your gates will always be open; *
　　by day or night they will never be shut.
They will call you, The City of the Lord, *
　　The Zion of the Holy One of Israel.
Violence will no more be heard in your land, *
　　ruin or destruction within your borders.
You will call your walls, Salvation, *
　　and all your portals, Praise.
The sun will no more be your light by day; *
　　by night you will not need the brightness of the moon.

The Lord will be your everlasting light, *
  and your God will be your glory.

Glory to the Father, and to the Son, and to the Holy Spirit: *
  as it was in the beginning, is now, and will be for ever. Amen.

12   A Song of Creation   *Benedicite, omnia opera Domini*
Song of the Three Young Men, 35-65

*One or more sections of this Canticle may be used. Whatever the
selection, it begins with the Invocation and concludes with the Doxology.*

Invocation

Glorify the Lord, all you works of the Lord, *
  praise him and highly exalt him for ever.
In the firmament of his power, glorify the Lord, *
  praise him and highly exalt him for ever.

I   The Cosmic Order

Glorify the Lord, you angels and all powers of the Lord, *
  O heavens and all waters above the heavens.
Sun and moon and stars of the sky, glorify the Lord, *
  praise him and highly exalt him for ever.

Glorify the Lord, every shower of rain and fall of dew, *
  all winds and fire and heat.
Winter and summer, glorify the Lord, *
  praise him and highly exalt him for ever.

Glorify the Lord, O chill and cold, *
  drops of dew and flakes of snow.
Frost and cold, ice and sleet, glorify the Lord, *
  praise him and highly exalt him for ever.

Glorify the Lord, O nights and days, *
   O shining light and enfolding dark.
Storm clouds and thunderbolts, glorify the Lord, *
   praise him and highly exalt him for ever.

II   *The Earth and its Creatures*

Let the earth glorify the Lord, *
   praise him and highly exalt him for ever.
Glorify the Lord, O mountains and hills,
and all that grows upon the earth, *
   praise him and highly exalt him for ever.

Glorify the Lord, O springs of water, seas, and streams, *
   O whales and all that move in the waters.
All birds of the air, glorify the Lord, *
   praise him and highly exalt him for ever.

Glorify the Lord, O beasts of the wild, *
   and all you flocks and herds.
O men and women everywhere, glorify the Lord, *
   praise him and highly exalt him for ever.

III   *The People of God*

Let the people of God glorify the Lord, *
   praise him and highly exalt him for ever.
Glorify the Lord, O priests and servants of the Lord, *
   praise him and highly exalt him for ever.

Glorify the Lord, O spirits and souls of the righteous, *
   praise him and highly exalt him for ever.
You that are holy and humble of heart, glorify the Lord, *
   praise him and highly exalt him for ever.

Doxology

Let us glorify the Lord: Father, Son, and Holy Spirit; *
   praise him and highly exalt him for ever.
In the firmament of his power, glorify the Lord, *
   praise him and highly exalt him for ever.

13   A Song of Praise   *Benedictus es, Domine*
Song of the Three Young Men, 29-34

Glory to you, Lord God of our fathers; *
   you are worthy of praise; glory to you.
Glory to you for the radiance of your holy Name; *
   we will praise you and highly exalt you for ever.

Glory to you in the splendor of your temple; *
   on the throne of your majesty, glory to you.
Glory to you, seated between the Cherubim; *
   we will praise you and highly exalt you for ever.

Glory to you, beholding the depths; *
   in the high vault of heaven, glory to you.
Glory to you, Father, Son, and Holy Spirit; *
   we will praise you and highly exalt you for ever.

14   A Song of Penitence   *Kyrie Pantokrator*
Prayer of Manasseh, 1-2, 4, 6-7, 11-15

Especially suitable in Lent, and on other penitential occasions

O Lord and Ruler of the hosts of heaven, *
   God of Abraham, Isaac, and Jacob,
   and of all their righteous offspring:
You made the heavens and the earth, *
   with all their vast array.

All things quake with fear at your presence; *
    they tremble because of your power.
But your merciful promise is beyond all measure; *
    it surpasses all that our minds can fathom.
O Lord, you are full of compassion, *
    long-suffering, and abounding in mercy.
You hold back your hand; *
    you do not punish as we deserve.
In your great goodness, Lord,
you have promised forgiveness to sinners, *
    that they may repent of their sin and be saved.
And now, O Lord, I bend the knee of my heart, *
    and make my appeal, sure of your gracious goodness.
I have sinned, O Lord, I have sinned, *
    and I know my wickedness only too well.
Therefore I make this prayer to you: *
    Forgive me, Lord, forgive me.
Do not let me perish in my sin, *
    nor condemn me to the depths of the earth.
For you, O Lord, are the God of those who repent, *
    and in me you will show forth your goodness.
Unworthy as I am, you will save me,
in accordance with your great mercy, *
    and I will praise you without ceasing all the days of my life.
For all the powers of heaven sing your praises, *
    and yours is the glory to ages of ages. Amen.

15   The Song of Mary   *Magnificat*
Luke 1:46-55

My soul proclaims the greatness of the Lord,
my spirit rejoices in God my Savior; *
    for he has looked with favor on his lowly servant.

15 The Song of Mary

This Canticle, known as the *Magnificat*, has a long history of Prayer Book use at Evening Prayer but traditionally has been used in the morning as well. St. Luke gives it as Mary's song at the Annunciation; it is modeled on Hannah's song (1 Samuel 2) and draws on other Old Testament sources as well.

16 The Song of Zechariah

Drawing again on Old Testament sources, St. Luke composed this Canticle as Zechariah's response of praise to the birth of John the Baptist. Since it has to do with the promise of redemption, it might be used before a New Testament reading, and the table of suggested Canticles recommends its use in that position on major holy days and Sundays.

17 The Song of Simeon

The third Canticle drawn from St. Luke is Simeon's response to the presentation of Christ in the Temple. It has a long history of use in the evening and has generally been placed after the second lesson at Evening Prayer. The 1979 Prayer Book provides it for Morning Prayer as well, and for Compline and at the end of the Burial Office.

From this day all generations will call me blessed: *
    the Almighty has done great things for me,
    and holy is his Name.
He has mercy on those who fear him *
    in every generation.
He has shown the strength of his arm, *
    he has scattered the proud in their conceit.
He has cast down the mighty from their thrones, *
    and has lifted up the lowly.
He has filled the hungry with good things, *
    and the rich he has sent away empty.
He has come to the help of his servant Israel, *
    for he has remembered his promise of mercy,
The promise he made to our fathers, *
    to Abraham and his children for ever.

Glory to the Father, and to the Son, and to the Holy Spirit: *
    as it was in the beginning, is now, and will be for ever. Amen.

16   The Song of Zechariah   *Benedictus Dominus Deus*
    Luke 1:68-79

Blessed be the Lord, the God of Israel; *
    he has come to his people and set them free.
He has raised up for us a mighty savior, *
    born of the house of his servant David.
Through his holy prophets he promised of old,
that he would save us from our enemies, *
    from the hands of all who hate us.
He promised to show mercy to our fathers *
    and to remember his holy covenant.
This was the oath he swore to our father Abraham, *
    to set us free from the hands of our enemies,
Free to worship him without fear, *
    holy and righteous in his sight
    all the days of our life.

You, my child, shall be called the prophet of the Most High, *
   for you will go before the Lord to prepare his way,
To give his people knowledge of salvation *
   by the forgiveness of their sins.
In the tender compassion of our God *
   the dawn from on high shall break upon us,
To shine on those who dwell in darkness and the
                           shadow of death, *
   and to guide our feet into the way of peace.

Glory to the Father, and to the Son, and to the Holy Spirit: *
   as it was in the beginning, is now, and will be for ever. Amen.

17   The Song of Simeon   *Nunc dimittis*
   Luke 2:29-32

Lord, you now have set your servant free *
   to go in peace as you have promised;
For these eyes of mine have seen the Savior, *
   whom you have prepared for all the world to see:
A Light to enlighten the nations, *
   and the glory of your people Israel.

Glory to the Father, and to the Son, and to the Holy Spirit: *
   as it was in the beginning, is now, and will be for ever. Amen.

18   A Song to the Lamb   *Dignus es*
   Revelation 4:11; 5:9-10, 13

Splendor and honor and kingly power *
   are yours by right, O Lord our God,
For you created everything that is, *
   and by your will they were created and have their being;

And yours by right, O Lamb that was slain, *
  for with your blood you have redeemed for God,
From every family, language, people, and nation, *
  a kingdom of priests to serve our God.

And so, to him who sits upon the throne, *
  and to Christ the Lamb,
Be worship and praise, dominion and splendor, *
  for ever and for evermore.

19 The Song of the Redeemed *Magna et mirabilia*
Revelation 15:3-4

O ruler of the universe, Lord God,
great deeds are they that you have done, *
  surpassing human understanding.
Your ways are ways of righteousness and truth, *
  O King of all the ages.

Who can fail to do you homage, Lord,
and sing the praises of your Name? *
  for you only are the Holy One.
All nations will draw near and fall down before you, *
  because your just and holy works have been revealed.

Glory to the Father, and to the Son, and to the Holy Spirit: *
  as it was in the beginning, is now, and will be for ever. Amen.

20 Glory to God *Gloria in excelsis*

Glory to God in the highest,
  and peace to his people on earth.

Lord God, heavenly King,
almighty God and Father,

we worship you, we give you thanks,
we praise you for your glory.

Lord Jesus Christ, only Son of the Father,
Lord God, Lamb of God,
you take away the sin of the world:
    have mercy on us;
you are seated at the right hand of the Father:
    receive our prayer.

For you alone are the Holy One,
you alone are the Lord,
you alone are the Most High,
    Jesus Christ,
    with the Holy Spirit,
    in the glory of God the Father. Amen.

21 **You are God** *Te Deum laudamus*

You are God: we praise you;
You are the Lord: we acclaim you;
You are the eternal Father:
All creation worships you.
To you all angels, all the powers of heaven,
Cherubim and Seraphim, sing in endless praise:
    Holy, holy, holy Lord, God of power and might,
    heaven and earth are full of your glory.
The glorious company of apostles praise you.
The noble fellowship of prophets praise you.
The white-robed army of martyrs praise you.
Throughout the world the holy Church acclaims you;
    Father, of majesty unbounded,
    your true and only Son, worthy of all worship,
    and the Holy Spirit, advocate and guide.

You, Christ, are the king of glory,
the eternal Son of the Father.
When you became man to set us free
you did not shun the Virgin's womb.
You overcame the sting of death
and opened the kingdom of heaven to all believers.
You are seated at God's right hand in glory.
We believe that you will come and be our judge.
  Come then, Lord, and help your people,
  bought with the price of your own blood,
  and bring us with your saints
  to glory everlasting.

The Apostles' Creed

Officiant and People together, all standing

I believe in God, the Father almighty,
  creator of heaven and earth.
I believe in Jesus Christ, his only Son, our Lord.
  He was conceived by the power of the Holy Spirit
    and born of the Virgin Mary.
  He suffered under Pontius Pilate,
    was crucified, died, and was buried.
  He descended to the dead.
  On the third day he rose again.
  He ascended into heaven,
    and is seated at the right hand of the Father.
  He will come again to judge the living and the dead.
I believe in the Holy Spirit,
  the holy catholic Church,
  the communion of saints,
  the forgiveness of sins,
  the resurrection of the body,
  and the life everlasting. Amen.

18 and 19 A Song to the Lamb and The Song of the Redeemed
Both of these Canticles may have been Christian hymns before they
were made part of the Book of Revelation. They have had only limited liturgical use and have not been included in previous Prayer
Books. As visions of heavenly praise, they form an appropriate
response to the New Testament readings, especially at festival times.

20 and 21 Glory to God and Te Deum
These are the only non-biblical Canticles and they can be traced back
to at least the fourth century. The *Gloria* has been an integral part of
the mass since the Middle Ages, but the first American Prayer Book
allowed it as an option in Morning Prayer and it is especially appropriate at Christmas time. The Te Deum (a nice legend tells us that it
was composed spontaneously by Ambrose and Augustine at
Augustine's baptism) has had various liturgical uses but has often
been set to music for occasions of great triumph such as a corona-
tion. It is especially appropriate for Sundays and major holy days.

The Apostles' Creed
Until this point, the only direction given about position is that all
should kneel for the Confession. An individual or small group might
remain seated for the psalms, lessons, and Canticles. But all should
stand for the Creed, as we move from the passive position of hearers
to the active position of doers. The Creed is our response to the readings and it is stated in words that Christians have recited since at
least the second century. Although we have no evidence for the legend that the apostles themselves wrote this Creed, each contributing
one phrase, we can demonstrate that each phrase of this Creed is
directly drawn from the Bible. This Creed is a summary of biblical
teaching; it teaches what the apostles taught. The Apostles' Creed
has always been closely associated with baptism: it is an individual's
statement of faith and reminds us always of the commitment made
in our baptism. The Nicene Creed, by contrast, is a corporate statement of the church's faith and begins with "We believe . . ."

The Prayers

The people stand or kneel

Officiant	The Lord be with you.
People	And also with you.
Officiant	Let us pray.

Officiant and People

Our Father, who art in heaven,
    hallowed be thy Name,
    thy kingdom come,
    thy will be done,
        on earth as it is in heaven.
Give us this day our daily bread.
And forgive us our trespasses,
    as we forgive those
        who trespass against us.
And lead us not into temptation,
    but deliver us from evil.
For thine is the kingdom,
    and the power, and the glory,
    for ever and ever. Amen.

Our Father in heaven,
    hallowed be your Name,
    your kingdom come,
    your will be done,
        on earth as in heaven.
Give us today our daily bread.
Forgive us our sins
    as we forgive those
        who sin against us.
Save us from the time of trial,
    and deliver us from evil.
For the kingdom, the power,
    and the glory are yours,
    now and for ever. Amen.

Then follows one of these sets of Suffrages

A

V.   Show us your mercy, O Lord;
R.   And grant us your salvation.
V.   Clothe your ministers with righteousness;
R.   Let your people sing with joy.
V.   Give peace, O Lord, in all the world;
R.   For only in you can we live in safety.

Just as the Nicene Creed was a late addition to the eucharist, so the Apostles' Creed was a late addition to the Daily Office. The Christian faith is best expressed not in words but in worship, mission, and service. The Creeds are a useful verbal summary of our faith, but words alone are never enough.

The Prayers

Prayer in the narrow sense is a very minor element in the service of Morning Prayer. The Lord's Prayer and three other brief prayers are the minimum provided, though many other prayers can be added, as indicated on page 101.

The Lord's Prayer is, of course, the basic prayer of Christians and is closely related to the central themes of this service. We hear in Scripture what God has done and has promised; therefore we pray, "Thy kingdom come, thy will be done." We have come to sanctify time; therefore we pray, "Give us this day our daily bread."

V. Lord, keep this nation under your care;
R. And guide us in the way of justice and truth.
V. Let your way be known upon earth;
R. Your saving health among all nations.
V. Let not the needy, O Lord, be forgotten;
R. Nor the hope of the poor be taken away.
V. Create in us clean hearts, O God;
R. And sustain us with your Holy Spirit.

B

V. Save your people, Lord, and bless your inheritance;
R. Govern and uphold them, now and always.
V. Day by day we bless you;
R. We praise your Name for ever.
V. Lord, keep us from all sin today;
R. Have mercy on us, Lord, have mercy.
V. Lord, show us your love and mercy;
R. For we put our trust in you.
V. In you, Lord, is our hope;
R. And we shall never hope in vain.

The Officiant then says one or more of the following Collects

The Collect of the Day

A Collect for Sundays

O God, you make us glad with the weekly remembrance of
the glorious resurrection of your Son our Lord: Give us this
day such blessing through our worship of you, that the week
to come may be spent in your favor; through Jesus Christ our
Lord. *Amen.*

The traditional version of the Lord's Prayer is based on the Great Bible of 1539, a revision of the first complete English-language Bible issued in 1535 by Miles Coverdale. Protestant churches generally use the King James Version of 1611 (with "debts" instead of "trespasses"), but Episcopalians and other Anglicans have always been reluctant to move to that or any newer version! The contemporary version is the work of the International Consultation on English Texts (ICET), an ecumenical committee created to provide modern texts that all churches can use in common. (*The Song of Zechariah, Glory to God, Song of Mary,* and *Te Deum* are also the work of the ICET.)

The versicles and responses after the Lord's Prayer are called "suffrages," a word related to suffragan bishop and suffragettes. The word has to do with help and assistance. These brief prayers ask God's help and assistance for ourselves, the church, the world, and those in need. Both sets of suffrages have medieval roots but are drawn (except the fourth versicle and response in set A) from the psalms. They are often called "The Lesser Litany" and are very similar in purpose to the prayers that follow.

A Collect for Fridays

Almighty God, whose most dear Son went not up to joy but first he suffered pain, and entered not into glory before he was crucified: Mercifully grant that we, walking in the way of the cross, may find it none other than the way of life and peace; through Jesus Christ your Son our Lord. *Amen.*

A Collect for Saturdays

Almighty God, who after the creation of the world rested from all your works and sanctified a day of rest for all your creatures: Grant that we, putting away all earthly anxieties, may be duly prepared for the service of your sanctuary, and that our rest here upon earth may be a preparation for the eternal rest promised to your people in heaven; through Jesus Christ our Lord. *Amen.*

A Collect for the Renewal of Life

O God, the King eternal, whose light divides the day from the night and turns the shadow of death into the morning: Drive far from us all wrong desires, incline our hearts to keep your law, and guide our feet into the way of peace; that, having done your will with cheerfulness during the day, we may, when night comes, rejoice to give you thanks; through Jesus Christ our Lord. *Amen.*

A Collect for Peace

O God, the author of peace and lover of concord, to know you is eternal life and to serve you is perfect freedom: Defend us, your humble servants, in all assaults of our enemies; that we, surely trusting in your defense, may not fear the power of any adversaries; through the might of Jesus Christ our Lord. *Amen.*

The Collects and Prayers

A collect (coll´ect) is a brief form of prayer that collects our thoughts around a single theme. The Collect for the Day may be used or one or more of the others. Although only three are assigned a particular day, there are seven collects given and one can be used on each day of the week. These collects are drawn from various sources, ranging from St. Augustine (a phrase in the Collect for Peace) to Archbishop Benson of Canterbury, 1882-1896 (A Collect for Saturdays).

One of three "prayers for mission" follows the collect(s). The first of these is an ancient part of the Good Friday liturgy while the second was written by a nineteenth century missionary bishop of Calcutta, and the third by Charles Henry Brent, who served as Bishop of the Philippines (1901-1918) and Western New York (1918-1929).

A hymn or anthem may be sung before the closing prayers. An "Office Hymn" was a usual part of the monastic service and has typically been an optional part of Morning Prayer.

The General Thanksgiving is believed to have been inspired by a private prayer of Queen Elizabeth I and was first included in the 1662 English Prayer Book. Said in unison, it provides a balance to the General Confession said at the beginning of the service. Its beautifully shaped phrases have made it one of the best-known and loved prayers in the Prayer Book. "The means of grace and . . . the hope of glory" is a powerful summary of the effects of Christ's ministry. The prayer moves from thankfulness for God's gifts to the need to give ourselves to God's service as we go out from this time of prayer.

A Collect for Grace

Lord God, almighty and everlasting Father, you have brought us in safety to this new day: Preserve us with your mighty power, that we may not fall into sin, nor be overcome by adversity; and in all we do, direct us to the fulfilling of your purpose; through Jesus Christ our Lord. *Amen.*

A Collect for Guidance

Heavenly Father, in you we live and move and have our being: We humbly pray you so to guide and govern us by your Holy Spirit, that in all the cares and occupations of our life we may not forget you, but may remember that we are ever walking in your sight; through Jesus Christ our Lord. *Amen.*

Then, unless the Eucharist or a form of general intercession is to follow, one of these prayers for mission is added

Almighty and everlasting God, by whose Spirit the whole body of your faithful people is governed and sanctified: Receive our supplications and prayers which we offer before you for all members of your holy Church, that in their vocation and ministry they may truly and devoutly serve you; through our Lord and Savior Jesus Christ. *Amen.*

or this

O God, you have made of one blood all the peoples of the earth, and sent your blessed Son to preach peace to those who are far off and to those who are near: Grant that people everywhere may seek after you and find you; bring the nations into your fold; pour out your Spirit upon all flesh; and hasten the coming of your kingdom; through Jesus Christ our Lord. *Amen.*

or the following

Lord Jesus Christ, you stretched out your arms of love on the hard wood of the cross that everyone might come within the reach of your saving embrace: So clothe us in your Spirit that we, reaching forth our hands in love, may bring those who do not know you to the knowledge and love of you; for the honor of your Name. *Amen.*

Here may be sung a hymn or anthem.

Authorized intercessions and thanksgivings may follow.

Before the close of the Office one or both of the following may be used

The General Thanksgiving

Officiant and People

Almighty God, Father of all mercies,
we your unworthy servants give you humble thanks
for all your goodness and loving-kindness
to us and to all whom you have made.
We bless you for our creation, preservation,
and all the blessings of this life;
but above all for your immeasurable love
in the redemption of the world by our Lord Jesus Christ;
for the means of grace, and for the hope of glory.
And, we pray, give us such an awareness of your mercies,
that with truly thankful hearts we may show forth your praise,
not only with our lips, but in our lives,
by giving up our selves to your service,
and by walking before you
in holiness and righteousness all our days;
through Jesus Christ our Lord,
to whom, with you and the Holy Spirit,
be honor and glory throughout all ages. Amen.

A Prayer of St. Chrysostom

Almighty God, you have given us grace at this time with one accord to make our common supplication to you; and you have promised through your well-beloved Son that when two or three are gathered together in his Name you will be in the midst of them: Fulfill now, O Lord, our desires and petitions as may be best for us; granting us in this world knowledge of your truth, and in the age to come life everlasting. *Amen.*

Then may be said

Let us bless the Lord.
Thanks be to God.

From Easter Day through the Day of Pentecost "Alleluia, alleluia" may be added to the preceding versicle and response.

The Officiant may then conclude with one of the following

The grace of our Lord Jesus Christ, and the love of God, and the fellowship of the Holy Spirit, be with us all evermore. *Amen.*   *2 Corinthians 13:14*

May the God of hope fill us with all joy and peace in believing through the power of the Holy Spirit. *Amen.*
Romans 15:13

Glory to God whose power, working in us, can do infinitely more than we can ask or imagine: Glory to him from generation to generation in the Church, and in Christ Jesus for ever and ever. *Amen.*   *Ephesians 3:20, 21*

A Prayer of St. Chrysostom (who died in the year 407) probably does not go back quite that far but has been used in the Greek liturgy from a very early date. It is based on Jesus' teaching in Matthew 18:20 and forms a fitting conclusion to the prayers.

"Let us bless the Lord," with the response "Thanks be to God," is a traditional conclusion of many services and is an option at the end of the eucharist as well.

As the service began, so it concludes with a verse from the Bible. Each of the three choices offered comes from a Pauline epistle, where it concludes the epistle itself (2 Corinthians) or the main body of teaching. Only the first sentence is Trinitarian, but the other two speak more specifically of the power at work within us to give us joy and peace and accomplish God's purpose.

Morning Prayer, Rite I

The Rite I form of Morning Prayer differs from Rite II primarily in using traditional rather than contemporary language. The sequence of Opening Sentences, Confession, Invitatory, Psalm, Lessons and Canticles, Creed, and Prayers is exactly the same, although there are some differences in the Canticles and prayers provided. For a general discussion of Morning Prayer, then, the material on pages 3-7 applies equally to both Rite I and Rite II. We will take time here only to comment on those few things that are different.

The same 33 verses of Scripture as Opening Sentences are provided for both rites. The first difference that may be noted is in the Invitation to the General Confession (page 41). This exhortation, essentially unchanged from 1552 to 1928, has been much shortened in both the Rite I and II versions. In both it lists the purposes for which we gather: to render thanks to God, to praise God, to hear God's word, and to offer prayer. Oddly, the Rite II version omits the first of these purposes: "to render thanks for the great benefits that we have received." Since both versions include the General Thanksgiving, this difference cannot be explained.

The forms of Confession and Absolution in Rites I and II are different, but both are based on very ancient models. The Rite I Confession omits the words "and there is no health in us" and "miserable offenders" found in earlier Prayer Books. The first of these phrases especially is questionable theology, since it seems to imply that there is no goodness left in us. Some theologians have taught that but Anglican theologians have normally maintained that the image of God remains present in every human being, though deformed or marred by sin.

The *Venite* has appeared in slightly different versions in different Prayer Books over the years. The first American Prayer Book dropped the last four and a half verses of Psalm 95 and added two verses from Psalm 96 in their place. The Rite II version drops the verses from Psalm 96 and adds the half-verse of Psalm 95, "Oh, that today you would hearken to his voice!" The effect is to make the Rite I version centered on God's holiness and worship, while the Rite II version ends with a challenge to the worshiper. The traditional (pre-1928) version of the Venite (Psalm 95 in the language of the Great Bible) is also made available on page 146 and, of course, the contemporary version can be found on page 724.

The Canticles provided for Morning Prayer, Rite I, are all those provided in the 1928 Prayer Book for Morning Prayer as well as those provided in that book for Evening Prayer: the *Magnificat*, the *Nunc Dimittis*, and *Gloria in excelsis*. The last named was provided in 1928 only as an alternative to the *Gloria Patri* at the end of the psalms but is given here as a Canticle, perhaps on the theory that everything in the 1928 Prayer Book should be included in the 1979 Prayer Book somewhere. The Canticles added to the 1979 Prayer Book (numbers 8, 9, 10, 11, 14, 18, and 19) have not been added to Rite I. Nevertheless any Rite II Canticle can be used with Rite I, and vice versa.

After the Creed and Lord's Prayer, the same two sets of versicles and responses are provided with, perhaps, one significant difference. The response to the last versicle in Set B in Rite II is "And we shall never hope in vain." Rite I, less optimistically, says only, "Let me never be confounded." The first verion is from the ICET; the latter follows more closely the biblical text of Psalm 71:1.

Of the prayers, only two seem significantly different. The Collect for Grace is very differently phrased in the two services, though the same general line of thought seems to be followed. The General Thanksgiving in Rite II is modified for the sake of inclusive language by changing "to us and to all men" to "to all whom you have made."

Holy Baptism

Holy Baptism

Introduction

Baptism has to do with identity, community, and eternal life. It is not simply a ceremony marking the beginning of church membership; it is far more radical than that. The service of Holy Baptism speaks of moving from darkness to light and from death to life.

Baptism has to do with identity. The one who is baptized is marked as belonging to God. Baptism is a way of saying that we know who we are: that we are made in God's image and called to belong to God forever.

Baptism has to do with community. The one who is baptized is brought into a new community: the church, which is the body of Christ. Baptism is a bond of unity among all those who belong to God.

Baptism has to do with life. The one who is baptized acknowledges human mortality and accepts the gift of new and eternal life in Christ. In baptism we are buried with Christ and raised to new life in him.

To say that baptism has to do with sin is to say the same things in another way. Sin is separation from God; therefore we are separated from the source of life, from each other, and even from our true selves. Baptism overcomes that separation and restores us to unity with God, brings us into the Christian community, and restores the image of God in us.

Concerning the Service

The directions on page 298 make some important statements, not simply about the service, but about the nature and meaning of baptism: first and foremost, that through it we receive full membership in the church, a relationship that cannot be dissolved. Baptism, in other words, needs no "completion" in confirmation, nor is there any need ever for anyone to be "rebaptized."

Second, baptism is always a corporate act; it has to do with membership in the church, and therefore the church should be assembled when there are candidates for baptism. Archbishop Thomas Cranmer stressed this principle in the first English Prayer Book, saying "it should not be ministered but upon Sundays and other holy days, when the most number of people may come together. As well for that the congregation there present may testify the receiving of them that be newly baptized, as also because in the baptism of infants, every man present may be put in remembrance of his own profession made to God in his baptism."

Third, baptism is normally to be set in the context of the eucharist, and therefore the shape of the service is that of the first part of the eucharist. Through most of the church's history, baptism has been ministered primarily at the Easter Vigil service or as a separate, often private, rite. Now baptism is brought into the center of the church's worship so that all may be frequently reminded of the new life into which we are called.

Finally, adult members of the church, parents or others, are to take responsibility for those newly baptized and see that the promises made in their name are carried out. The role of Godparents should not be seen as an honorary position. Serious commitments are made—and should not be made by those unable or unwilling to keep them. If the parents are unable to provide such individuals, the congregation might well appoint sponsors or Godparents from its own membership.

The "Additional Directions" at the end of the service suggest that the Presentation of the Candidates might not take place at the font and that a procession to the font may then occur just before the Thanksgiving over the Water. A procession to the font adds a sense of movement from the old life to the new, and a procession to the front of the church after the baptism symbolizes movement into the gathered life of the Christian community.

A candle (often a small replica of the Paschal Candle) may be given to those newly baptized as a symbol of the light of Christ that they will now carry through life.

Holy Baptism

A hymn, psalm, or anthem may be sung.

The people standing, the Celebrant says

> Blessed be God: Father, Son, and Holy Spirit.

People And blessed be his kingdom, now and for ever. Amen.

In place of the above, from Easter Day through the Day of Pentecost

Celebrant Alleluia. Christ is risen.
People The Lord is risen indeed. Alleluia.

In Lent and on other penitential occasions

Celebrant Bless the Lord who forgives all our sins.
People His mercy endures for ever.

The Celebrant then continues

> There is one Body and one Spirit;

People There is one hope in God's call to us;
Celebrant One Lord, one Faith, one Baptism;
People One God and Father of all.

Celebrant The Lord be with you.
People And also with you.
Celebrant Let us pray.

Holy Baptism

Commentary

Since baptism is ordinarily to be incorporated into the eucharist, the service begins in the same way as the eucharist on a normal day. The priest and people greet each other with words appropriate to the season. Since, however, baptism is not recommended for penitential seasons, the third verse and response are unlikely to be used.

The usual opening verse and response are extended with a verse from the Epistle to the Ephesians (4:4-6a) indicating to all that this service is to include a baptism or baptisms. The verse also sums up the meaning of baptism: we are brought into one Body to share one life as children of one God.

The Collect of the Day

People   Amen.

At the principal service on a Sunday or other feast, the Collect and Lessons are properly those of the Day. On other occasions they are selected from "At Baptism." (See Additional Directions, page 312.)

The Lessons

The people sit. One or two Lessons, as appointed, are read, the Reader first saying

A Reading (Lesson) from _____ .

A citation giving chapter and verse may be added.

After each Reading, the Reader may say

The Word of the Lord.
People   Thanks be to God.

or the Reader may say   Here ends the Reading (Epistle).

Silence may follow.

A Psalm, hymn, or anthem may follow each Reading.

Then, all standing, the Deacon or a Priest reads the Gospel, first saying

The Holy Gospel of our Lord Jesus Christ
according to _____ .
People   Glory to you, Lord Christ.

After the Gospel, the Reader says

The Gospel of the Lord.
People   Praise to you, Lord Christ.

The Collect and Lessons

The beginning of the eucharist is shortened by omitting the Kyrie or Gloria and proceeding directly to the Collect for the Day. The lessons then follow. Unless for some very special reason the baptism does not take place at the parish eucharist, the lessons are those of the day. Such lessons, however, will not be inappropriate. Since the Bible is the foundation book of the Christian life, there are few if any passages that do not bear on the baptized life in some way. The sermon will easily be able to establish connections between the readings and the baptism, drawing out for the benefit of all those involved and the whole congregation what the lessons tell us about the gift of life that God pours out on the church.

The Sermon

Or the Sermon may be preached after the Peace.

Presentation and Examination of the Candidates

The Celebrant says

The Candidate(s) for Holy Baptism will now be presented.

Adults and Older Children

The candidates who are able to answer for themselves are presented individually by their Sponsors, as follows

Sponsor   I present N. to receive the Sacrament of Baptism.

The Celebrant asks each candidate when presented

      Do you desire to be baptized?
Candidate I do.

Infants and Younger Children

Then the candidates unable to answer for themselves are presented individually by their Parents and Godparents, as follows

Parents and Godparents

I present N. to receive the Sacrament of Baptism.

Presentation and Examination of the Candidates

Through the sermon, the service is not very different from that of a normal Sunday. Now, where the Creed would usually follow and express the belief of those present in the faith that has been proclaimed in the readings and sermon, the candidates for baptism are now presented. Baptism expresses in action what the Creed expresses in words.

The candidates are presented by others; even adults do not present themselves. The assumption is that the adult candidate has been instructed by church members who now attest to the candidate's faith. In the early days of the church, this "catechetical" process normally took three years. Today many parishes are restoring the practice of admitting candidates for baptism as "catechumens" and assigning them sponsors from the congregation to instruct them in the faith over an extended period of time. Adults are presented first because adult baptism is the normal procedure. Baptism of children is always abnormal in the sense that they cannot make the response of faith and must have others delegated to do it for them. It is especially in the baptism of adults that members of the congregation can be reminded of the significance of this life-changing act, an act that may not have made so great an impact on their own lives if they were baptized as infants.

Adult candidates for baptism must also express a desire for baptism. Notice that they are not asked to express their faith; they cannot know the full meaning of faith from outside the body of Christ. They can desire it, but they will learn its full meaning only after they are baptized.

When all have been presented the Celebrant asks the parents and godparents

Will you be responsible for seeing that the child you present is brought up in the Christian faith and life?

Parents and Godparents

I will, with God's help.

Celebrant

Will you by your prayers and witness help this child to grow into the full stature of Christ?

Parents and Godparents

I will, with God's help.

Then the Celebrant asks the following questions of the candidates who can speak for themselves, and of the parents and godparents who speak on behalf of the infants and younger children

Question Do you renounce Satan and all the spiritual forces of wickedness that rebel against God?

Answer I renounce them.

Question Do you renounce the evil powers of this world which corrupt and destroy the creatures of God?

Answer I renounce them.

Question Do you renounce all sinful desires that draw you from the love of God?

Answer I renounce them.

Question Do you turn to Jesus Christ and accept him as your Savior?

Answer I do.

Question Do you put your whole trust in his grace and love?
Answer I do.

If an infant is to be baptized, obviously no personal response of faith is possible. Therefore, others must speak on behalf of the child and take on the responsibility of seeing that the child does learn to understand and respond to the Christian faith. Godparents and parents are asked to commit themselves to seeing that the child they present is "brought up in the Christian faith and life" and to pray for the child and witness to the faith by their own lives.

When the parents and Godparents have made this commitment, they are in a position to speak for the child. In response to the next six questions, adult candidates speak for themselves while parents and Godparents speak for those unable to respond. The questions come in two groups: first, a threefold renunciation of evil; second, a threefold commitment to Jesus Christ as Savior. In earlier days, the response to these two groups of questions was often dramatized by having the candidates face the west when they renounced evil and then turn to the east, the place where the dawn breaks with new light and from which it was supposed the Savior would come again, to promise to follow Christ as Lord.

It is worth noticing that two of the three renunciations have to do with external forces of evil, and only the last with the evil within each of us. We live in a society that is becoming increasingly aware of the limits of individual human effort and the way in which our best efforts can be undone by powers beyond our control. To say we will not obey those powers is a first step; to join the community in which God's grace is at work is the second critical step toward overcoming the power of evil in human life.

Question	Do you promise to follow and obey him as your Lord?
Answer	I do.

When there are others to be presented, the Bishop says

The other Candidate(s) will now be presented.

Presenters	I present *these persons* for Confirmation.
or	I present *these persons* to be received into this Communion.
or	I present *these persons* who *desire* to reaffirm *their* baptismal vows.

The Bishop asks the candidates

Do you reaffirm your renunciation of evil?

Candidate I do.

Bishop

Do you renew your commitment to Jesus Christ?

Candidate

I do, and with God's grace I will follow him as my Savior and Lord.

After all have been presented, the Celebrant addresses the congregation, saying

Will you who witness these vows do all in your
power to support *these persons* in *their* life in Christ?

People   We will.

The Celebrant then says these or similar words

Let us join with *those* who *are* committing *themselves* to Christ
and renew our own baptismal covenant.

The Order for Holy Baptism also provides an opportunity to present candidates to be confirmed, to be received from another Communion, and to reaffirm their faith. Each of these groups or individuals is asked to reaffirm their renunciation of evil and renew their commitment to Christ.

Confirmation (which, with the other forms for reception or for renewing commitment, is also separately provided for on pages 413 ff.) developed in the Middle Ages as a separate stage in the process of Christian initiation. Those who had been baptized as infants were brought later to the bishop to be anointed with oil, a rite that had once been the final stage of the baptismal service itself. Gradually, this rite came to be seen as the "completion" of baptism and as a separate conferring of the Holy Spirit. It also became an opportunity for candidates to take upon themselves the promises their Godparents had made for them in baptism. Whether this rite still has a separate value is much debated, but it has deep roots in Anglican tradition.

Those who have been baptized and confirmed by a bishop of another church who wish to become members of the Episcopal Church need not be reconfirmed. They are presented to the bishop, who prays for them and welcomes them into the Episcopal Church.

Since many people wander away from active church membership at some point in their lives, the opportunity is given to mark a reawakened faith with a public act of commitment. This is a new provision that has been welcomed as a valuable addition in many parishes.

The congregation is then asked to support the candidates and invited to renew their own baptismal covenant.

The Baptismal Covenant

Celebrant Do you believe in God the Father?
People I believe in God, the Father almighty,
　　　　　creator of heaven and earth.

Celebrant Do you believe in Jesus Christ, the Son of God?
People I believe in Jesus Christ, his only Son, our Lord.
　　　　　He was conceived by the power of the Holy Spirit
　　　　　　and born of the Virgin Mary.
　　　　　He suffered under Pontius Pilate,
　　　　　　was crucified, died, and was buried.
　　　　　He descended to the dead.
　　　　　On the third day he rose again.
　　　　　He ascended into heaven,
　　　　　　and is seated at the right hand of the Father.
　　　　　He will come again to judge the living and the dead.

Celebrant Do you believe in God the Holy Spirit?
People I believe in the Holy Spirit,
　　　　　the holy catholic Church,
　　　　　the communion of saints,
　　　　　the forgiveness of sins,
　　　　　the resurrection of the body,
　　　　　and the life everlasting.

Celebrant Will you continue in the apostles' teaching and
fellowship, in the breaking of bread, and in the
prayers?
People I will, with God's help.

Celebrant Will you persevere in resisting evil, and, whenever
you fall into sin, repent and return to the Lord?
People I will, with God's help.

The Baptismal Covenant

Among the values of this Prayer Book is its renewed emphasis on the central role of baptism in Christian life. The early church gave it a central place, and the leaders of the Reformation in both England and Germany sought to restore that position. The first English Prayer Book said that baptisms should take place on Sunday so that all could be reminded of the commitment made in their own baptism. In keeping with that understanding, the whole congregation is now given opportunity to renew their own baptismal promises whenever a baptism takes place.

The Creeds were first developed as baptismal statements and the Apostles' Creed continues to serve as the chief individual statement of faith. In the early days of the church, the Creed was spoken by the candidate for baptism in response to three questions, as it is here. The candidate would have been immersed after each response.

A series of five questions has been added to the Creed, but notice that the only statement of faith made is the Creed itself; there are no other doctrines that must be accepted. The remaining questions have to do with the consequences of the Christian faith in daily life. The first question quotes a verse in the Book of Acts (2.42) that describes the life of the early church and asks whether the candidate will also follow that pattern. The remaining questions move from the continuing need for repentance to the need to proclaim the gospel, to serve others, and to work for justice, peace, and human dignity. The corporate dimension of Christian faith is given appropriate emphasis throughout this Prayer Book. The Christian life is not an individual matter, a "me and God" relationship, but a matter of membership in a body and of witness and service. It is valuable to be reminded of that whenever there is a baptism.

Celebrant	Will you proclaim by word and example the Good News of God in Christ?
People	I will, with God's help.
Celebrant	Will you seek and serve Christ in all persons, loving your neighbor as yourself?
People	I will, with God's help.
Celebrant	Will you strive for justice and peace among all people, and respect the dignity of every human being?
People	I will, with God's help.

Prayers for the Candidates

The Celebrant then says to the congregation

Let us now pray for *these persons* who *are* to receive the Sacrament of new birth [and for those (this person) who *have* renewed *their* commitment to Christ.]

A Person appointed leads the following petitions

Leader	Deliver *them*, O Lord, from the way of sin and death.
People	Lord, hear our prayer.
Leader	Open *their hearts* to your grace and truth.
People	Lord, hear our prayer.
Leader	Fill *them* with your holy and life-giving Spirit.
People	Lord, hear our prayer.
Leader	Keep *them* in the faith and communion of your holy Church.
People	Lord, hear our prayer.
Leader	Teach *them* to love others in the power of the Spirit.
People	Lord, hear our prayer.

Prayers for the Candidates

The priest now invites the congregation to pray for those who are being baptized or renewing their commitment to Christ. The prayers that follow were composed for this Prayer Book and may appropriately be led by one of the Godparents or another friend or relative of one of the candidates. The pronoun *them* in italics may be changed to *him* or *her,* but might also, if there are not too many candidates, be changed to the names of the candidates, at least in the first petition.

Notice how logically the petitions move, like the previous series of questions, from deliverance from sin to witness and service. First, God is asked to *deliver* the candidates from sin and death, then to *open* their hearts, then to *fill* what has been opened, then to *keep* what has been filled. Those who have come this far can then be *taught,* and when they are taught they can be *sent* to others. Then, at last, they can be *brought* into God's kingdom.

| *Leader* | Send *them* into the world in witness to your love. |
| *People* | Lord, hear our prayer. |

| *Leader* | Bring *them* to the fullness of your peace and glory. |
| *People* | Lord, hear our prayer. |

The Celebrant says

Grant, O Lord, that all who are baptized into the death
of Jesus Christ your Son may live in the power of his
resurrection and look for him to come again in glory; who
lives and reigns now and for ever. *Amen.*

Thanksgiving over the Water

The Celebrant blesses the water, first saying

The Lord be with you.

People And also with you.

Celebrant Let us give thanks to the Lord our God.

People It is right to give him thanks and praise.

Celebrant

We thank you, Almighty God, for the gift of water.
Over it the Holy Spirit moved in the beginning of creation.
Through it you led the children of Israel out of their bondage
in Egypt into the land of promise. In it your Son Jesus
received the baptism of John and was anointed by the Holy
Spirit as the Messiah, the Christ, to lead us, through his death
and resurrection, from the bondage of sin into everlasting life.

We thank you, Father, for the water of Baptism. In it we are
buried with Christ in his death. By it we share in his
resurrection. Through it we are reborn by the Holy Spirit.
Therefore in joyful obedience to your Son, we bring into his

The closing collect introduces two central themes for the first time: death and resurrection, and the second coming. That baptism involves death and resurrection can be forgotten if water is simply poured over the individual's forehead. That action looks like washing and puts the emphasis on being cleansed from sin. Baptism by immersion is preferable but not always practical. When baptism is so done, it is clear that something more radical is involved: the individual is buried in the water not merely to be washed of sin, but to die to sin and then be raised to a new life in Christ.

Thanksgiving over the Water

Although the early church believed that all water had been sanctified by the baptism of Christ in the Jordan, prayers for the blessing of the baptismal water began to be said very early in the life of the church. By the Middle Ages, the prayers and ceremonies over the water had become very elaborate, and Cranmer, like the continental reformers, simplified this part of the service. A prayer for the blessing of the water has, however, remained a strong part of the Anglican tradition, and it has often been modelled on the eucharistic prayer.

The traditional prayers for the blessing of the water have, as this prayer does, usually made reference to many of the ways in which God has used water to cleanse and renew the world. The waters of Creation, the rivers of Eden, the flood, the Red Sea, the water from the side of Christ, and so on, have typically been remembered here. Some of these are mentioned in this prayer, which goes on to give thanks for the water of baptism in which we share Christ's death and resurrection and the gift of the Holy Spirit.

fellowship those who come to him in faith, baptizing them in the Name of the Father, and of the Son, and of the Holy Spirit.

At the following words, the Celebrant touches the water

Now sanctify this water, we pray you, by the power of your Holy Spirit, that those who here are cleansed from sin and born again may continue for ever in the risen life of Jesus Christ our Savior.

To him, to you, and to the Holy Spirit, be all honor and glory, now and for ever. *Amen.*

Consecration of the Chrism

The Bishop may then consecrate oil of Chrism, placing a hand on the vessel of oil, and saying

Eternal Father, whose blessed Son was anointed by the Holy Spirit to be the Savior and servant of all, we pray you to consecrate this oil, that those who are sealed with it may share in the royal priesthood of Jesus Christ; who lives and reigns with you and the Holy Spirit, for ever and ever. *Amen.*

The Baptism

Each candidate is presented by name to the Celebrant, or to an assisting priest or deacon, who then immerses, or pours water upon, the candidate, saying

N., I baptize you in the Name of the Father, and of the Son, and of the Holy Spirit. *Amen.*

Consecration of the Chrism

In Jewish practice, kings and priests were anointed with oil when they were set apart for their offices, and the use of oil in baptism began very early. The one baptized is joined in the body of those who share the kingship and priesthood of Jesus who is the Christ, the anointed one.

The bishop may bless oil for the anointing when he or she comes to visit a parish, but the oil is more often blessed at the cathedral during Holy Week and distributed to the clergy at that time for use in baptism. This prayer, then, is usually omitted.

The Baptism

At one time, names were given in baptism, but the original custom, now restored, was for candidates to be presented by name. It is Christ's name that is given to us in baptism, not our own.

Notice again that the Prayer Book, as it has always done, mentions baptism by immersion first. Long after the Reformation, this remained the normal practice and was altered only if the infant was thought to be too weak to endure such exposure. Unfortunately, many churches have fonts too small for immersion, but newer churches are once again being built with fonts large enough to make immersion possible. Where that has been done, we are able to see the true meaning of baptism: burial beneath the waters and resurrection to a new life.

Let us pray.

Heavenly Father, we thank you that by water and the Holy Spirit you have bestowed upon *these* your *servants* the forgiveness of sin, and have raised *them* to the new life of grace. Sustain *them,* O Lord, in your Holy Spirit. Give *them* an inquiring and discerning heart, the courage to will and to persevere, a spirit to know and to love you, and the gift of joy and wonder in all your works. *Amen.*

Then the Bishop or Priest places a hand on the person's head, marking on the forehead the sign of the cross [using Chrism if desired] and saying to each one

N., you are sealed by the Holy Spirit in Baptism and marked as Christ's own for ever. *Amen.*

Or this action may be done immediately after the administration of the water and before the preceding prayer.

When all have been baptized, the Celebrant says

Let us welcome the newly baptized.

Celebrant and People

We receive you into the household of God. Confess the faith of Christ crucified, proclaim his resurrection, and share with us in his eternal priesthood.

If Confirmation, Reception, or the Reaffirmation of Baptismal Vows is not to follow, the Peace is now exchanged

Celebrant The peace of the Lord be always with you.
People   And also with you.

The relationship between baptism and confirmation has been mentioned earlier. The artificial division between a water baptism for forgiveness of sin and the gift of the Spirit for strength to live a Christian life distorts the meaning of Christian initiation and creates the idea that confirmation is necessary for full church membership. The postbaptismal prayer makes it clear that the Holy Spirit is given in baptism. The gifts of the Spirit listed in the first prayer on page 308 are drawn from an ancient baptismal prayer based on Isaiah 11:2. This prayer is to be said "in full sight" of the congregation; so, if a baptistery not fully visible to the whole congregation is used, the prayer is not said until all have returned to the main body of the church.

The sign of the cross is made on the forehead (using oil blessed by the bishop if desired). Marking the person's forehead is a custom that may be traced back into Judaism, where converts were baptized and then marked with the Taw, the last letter of the Hebrew alphabet, as a symbol of the name of God. The sign is like a brand signifying ownership: the one baptized now belongs to God forever.

The welcome of the newly baptized is expressed both in word and act. The congregation expresses a welcome that also invites the new member to share in its witness and worship. The Peace here has special meaning; in fact, it is quite possible that the Peace first became part of Christian liturgy at baptisms. In the early church, those who were not baptized had to leave the eucharist before the Peace was shared. Thus the sharing of the Peace is a special privilege of the baptized through which they express their unity in Christ.

At Confirmation, Reception, or Reaffirmation

The Bishop says to the congregation

Let us now pray for *these persons* who *have* renewed *their* commitment to Christ.

Silence may be kept.

Then the Bishop says

Almighty God, we thank you that by the death and resurrection of your Son Jesus Christ you have overcome sin and brought us to yourself, and that by the sealing of your Holy Spirit you have bound us to your service. Renew in *these* your *servants* the covenant you made with *them* at *their* Baptism. Send *them* forth in the power of that Spirit to perform the service you set before *them*; through Jesus Christ your Son our Lord, who lives and reigns with you and the Holy Spirit, one God, now and for ever. *Amen.*

For Confirmation

The Bishop lays hands upon each one and says

Strengthen, O Lord, your servant *N.* with your Holy Spirit; empower *him* for your service; and sustain *him* all the days of *his* life. *Amen.*

or this

Defend, O Lord, your servant *N.* with your heavenly grace, that *he* may continue yours for ever, and daily increase in your Holy Spirit more and more, until *he* comes to your everlasting kingdom. *Amen.*

For Reception

N., we recognize you as a member of the one holy catholic and apostolic Church, and we receive you into the fellowship of this Communion. God, the Father, Son, and Holy Spirit, bless, preserve, and keep you. *Amen.*

For Reaffirmation

N., may the Holy Spirit, who has begun a good work in you, direct and uphold you in the service of Christ and his kingdom. *Amen.*

Then the Bishop says

Almighty and everliving God, let your fatherly hand ever be over *these* your *servants*; let your Holy Spirit ever be with *them*; and so lead *them* in the knowledge and obedience of your Word, that *they* may serve you in this life, and dwell with you in the life to come; through Jesus Christ our Lord. *Amen.*

The Peace is then exchanged

Bishop   The peace of the Lord be always with you.
People   And also with you.

At the Eucharist

The service then continues with the Prayers of the People or the Offertory of the Eucharist, at which the Bishop, when present, should be the principal Celebrant.

Except on Principal Feasts, the Proper Preface of Baptism may be used.

Alternative Ending

If there is no celebration of the Eucharist, the service continues with the Lord's Prayer

Our Father, who art in heaven,
    hallowed be thy Name,
    thy kingdom come,
    thy will be done,
        on earth as it is in heaven.
Give us this day our daily bread.
And forgive us our trespasses,
    as we forgive those
        who trespass against us.
And lead us not into temptation,
    but deliver us from evil.
For thine is the kingdom,
    and the power, and the glory,
        for ever and ever. Amen.

Our Father in heaven,
    hallowed be your Name,
    your kingdom come,
    your will be done,
        on earth as in heaven.
Give us today our daily bread.
Forgive us our sins
    as we forgive those
        who sin against us.
Save us from the time of trial
    and deliver us from evil.
For the kingdom, the power,
    and the glory are yours,
        now and for ever. Amen.

The Celebrant then says

All praise and thanks to you, most merciful Father, for adopting us as your own children, for incorporating us into your holy Church, and for making us worthy to share in the inheritance of the saints in light; through Jesus Christ your Son our Lord, who lives and reigns with you and the Holy Spirit, one God, for ever and ever. *Amen.*

Alms may be received and presented, and other prayers may be added, concluding with this prayer

Almighty God, the Father of our Lord Jesus Christ, from whom every family in heaven and earth is named, grant you to be strengthened with might by his Holy Spirit, that, Christ dwelling in your hearts by faith, you may be filled with all the fullness of God. *Amen.*

Normally, the eucharist follows the sharing of the Peace. The forms for confirmation, reception, and reaffirmation are provided on the next pages (309-310) but would come before the Peace if they are used.

An alternative ending is provided on page 311 if, in exceptional circumstances, the baptism is not part of the eucharist. The Lord's Prayer is included here since it is a part of every Prayer Book service and would be included if the eucharist does not follow.

The prayer that follows the Lord's Prayer is a much shortened version of a prayer found first in the 1552 Prayer Book. Only here is the concept of baptism as adoption mentioned, but it is an image used five times in the New Testament epistles; it refers back to Israel's adoption and forward to our final resurrection, as well as to the action of baptism. We are created in the image of God but become members of God's own family, the sons and daughters of God, only through baptism which may be seen, then, as an adoption ceremony.

The final prayer, like the opening dialogue on page 299, draws on the Epistle to the Ephesians (this time from 3:15-17), where the Fatherhood of God in relation to the family given God's name is mentioned. This concluding prayer is offered for all those present, that they may be strengthened by the Holy Spirit and that Christ may dwell in their hearts by faith.

Glossary

Antiphon: Sentences, usually from Scripture, said or sung before and after the psalms and Canticles in the Daily Offices.

Antiphonal: A method of reciting the psalms: verses are said or sung alternately by two groups.

Apocrypha: The word comes from a Greek word meaning "hidden." The Apocryphal books of the Bible were not written in Hebrew and therefore were not included in the Hebrew Bible. They were, nonetheless, part of the Bible used in the Greek-speaking world and therefore known and used by the early Christian Church. At the time of the Reformation, these books were excluded from the Bible, though most of them were included by Luther as an appendix. The Church of England included them in the Bible separately from other Old Testament books and said they were not to be used to establish doctrine.

Baptism: A symbolic washing with water used in Judaism for initiation and purification ceremonies. John the Baptist used it to prepare for the coming of the Messiah. In Christianity it has a range of meanings from sacramental rebirth to a symbolic affirmation of faith. See also the definitions on pages 29 and 858 of the Book of Common Prayer.

Canticle: The word comes from the Latin word for a song. Canticles are texts used in the Daily Offices and drawn from Biblical and post-biblical sources.

Chrysostom, St. John (c. 347-407): Patriarch of Constantinople and a great orator. The word "chrysostom" means "silver-tongued." He was often exiled because of his plain speaking about corruption in the church and court. The so-called "Prayer of St. Chrysostom" was probably composed after his death. Cranmer discovered it in the Greek liturgy and brought it into the Prayer Book

Collect: A short form of prayer (accent on the first syllable) with an invocation, petition, and ascription. The term is most often used of the theme prayer which comes just before the lessons in the eucharist.

Compline: The last of the ancient monastic offices, it was included in the Prayer Book of 1979.

Confirmation: The service which developed in the middle ages when bishops were unable to be present at baptisms. The sealing with oil and laying on of hands were delayed until the bishop could come and came to be thought of as a separate sacrament conferring the Holy Spirit. To "confirm" is to strengthen. Confirmation may be thought of as a sacrament to strengthen the candidate or (more commonly in churches which give less importance to sacraments) as the candidate's renewal of baptismal promises.

Cranmer, Thomas (1489-1556): Archbishop of Canterbury during the years when the English Church regained its independence from the Church of Rome. Cranmer edited the first English language Prayer Book and wrote many if its best-known prayers.

Creed: A statement of faith. The word comes from the Latin "credo" which means "I believe." The shorter, Apostles' Creed is a personal statement and therefore used at baptisms. The longer, Nicene Creed, is a corporate statement beginning, therefore, with the word "we."

Direct recitation: In this method of saying the psalms, they are sung or said in unison.

Eucharist: An ancient name for the communion service. The word means "thanksgiving." See also the definitions on pages 13 and 859-60.

Gloria in excelsis: An expanded version of the song sung by the angels announcing the birth of Christ. It has been used at least since the fourth century.

Gloria Patri: An ascription of praise added to the psalms as early as the fourth century.

Godparent: One who presents a child for baptism and makes commitments on behalf of the child. Oddly, the Prayer Book alternates between spelling this word with an upper case and lower case "g."

Guilbert, Charles (1908-): The Custodian of the Book of Common Prayer; his duty is to certify that all editions of the Book of Common Prayer conform to the officially authorized text.

Immersion: In baptism by immersion, the candidate is lowered under the water completely in a symbolic burial and resurrection.

Invitatory: The Canticle at the beginning of the first Office of the day which invites to prayer. The original Invitatory Canticle was Psalm 95 but others are now used as well.

Lauds: The traditional morning office of the western church. The word means "praise."

Liturgy: The Greek word means "public work." The worship of God is the public work of Christians and all formal worship can be referred to as liturgy. Often the term is used specifically of the eucharist.

Mattins: The midnight office of monastic orders, it was combined with Prime by Cranmer to form Morning Prayer and the title is often still used of that service.

None: The monastic office for the ninth hour.

Office: One of the daily round of monastic or Prayer Book services composed primarily of psalms, readings and prayers. The word means "duty."

Paschal: This word, from the Greek word for "Passover," refers to Easter. A paschal candle is often lit at the Easter Vigil and kept burning through the fifty days of Easter. The paschal candle may also be placed near the font and lit at baptisms. A small replica is sometimes given to someone newly baptized.

Prime: The monastic office appointed for the first hour of the day or 6 a.m.

Responsorial recitation: One of four methods of reciting the psalms recommended in the Prayer Book (p. 582). In this method, psalms are sung by a solo voice while choir and congregation sing a refrain.

Responsive recitation: This is probably the most common method of saying the psalms in the Episcopal Church: the leader and congregation alternate saying the verses or half verses.

Rite (ritual): The form of words used in a service. The word is often mis-used to refer to the ceremonies which accompany the words.

Sacrament: An outward and visible sign of an inward and spiritual grace; an effectual sign; an act which accomplishes what it signifies; a means by which God acts in human life through material signs.

Sext: The monastic office for the sixth hour of the day or noon.

Sponsor: One who presents a candidate for baptism and may have been responsible for instructing the candidate in the faith.

Terce: The monastic office for the third hour of the day

Venite: The Latin name for the 95th Psalm from its first word, "Come." In the Prayer Book it is sometimes shortened and in former Prayer Books has also included verses 9 and 13 of Psalm 96.

Vespers: The monastic office traditionally recited late in the afternoon or just after dark.

Vigil: A nighttime service, often ending with the eucharist, before a Sunday or saint's day and, especially, before Easter. The Prayer Book also provides a vigil for Pentecost.

Suggestions for Further Reading

Hatchett, Marion, *Commentary on the American Prayer Book*, New York, Seabury Press, 1980. This is the standard reference work for the 1979 Book of Common Prayer and the place where answers to most questions about it will be found.

Other books that might be helpful to a deeper understanding of baptism, liturgical worship, and the Anglican tradition include the following. Some of these books are out of print and most are not likely to be in your local library, but a good parish library should have them and a parish priest may be willing to loan them to those who care enough to ask.

On worship in general:

Dix, Dom Gregory, *The Shape of the Liturgy*, London, Dacre Press, 1945. A classic history of the development of the liturgy from its Jewish origins to the twentieth century; beautifully written, but also somewhat dated and more detailed than many people will want.

Price, Charles, and Weil, Louis, *Liturgy for Living*, New York, Seabury Press, 1979. One chapter on the meaning of worship, one on the history of the Prayer Book, one on baptism, and then several chapters about the various sections of the Prayer Book; this was written for the ordinary church member and provides a good introduction.

Otto, Rudolf, *The Idea of the Holy*, New York, Oxford University Press, 1950. This is one of the great books on the thoughts and feelings that underlie the human response to God.

Shepherd, Massey, *The Oxford American Prayer Book Commentary*, New York, Oxford University Press, 1950. This commentary is based on the 1928 Prayer Book and provides a facing page of commentary for every page of text for the whole book except the Psalter. While obviously out of date, it is still a helpful source of information and easy to use because of the format.

Underhill, Evelyn, *Worship*, New York, Harper and Brothers, 1936. A well-written history of the development of patterns of worship from primitive societies to the twentieth century written by an English woman sixty years ago but still a good place to begin.

On baptism in particular:

Every, George, *The Baptismal Sacrifice*, London, SCM Press, 1959. Baptism in relationship to sacrifice and the eucharist in history and contemporary society.

Robinson, J.A.T., *The Body*, London, SCM Press, 1952. Not easy reading, but there are few better discussions of what it means to be a member of Christ's body.

Stevick, Daniel, *Baptismal Moments; Baptismal Meanings*, New York, Church Hymnal Corporation*. History, theology, and the meaning of baptism in contemporary culture. New and useful.

Merriman, Michael, W., (ed.), *Baptismal Mystery and the Catechumenate*, New York, Church Hymnal Corporation*. A collection of essays, practical and theoretical, on various aspects of the catechumenate as it is being rediscovered by various churches.

Meyers, Ruth A. (ed.), *Baptism and Ministry*, New York, Church Hymnal Corporation*. A collection of recent essays on baptism and ministry.

*Now known as Church Publishing.

Index